Tim Westrom helps us understand that when our heart's desire (that which consumes us) is prayer that is consistent with the mind of Jesus (in effect praying in His name), that becomes a perpetual prayer that promises an anointing (the fruit of the Spirit). That thought alone is worth the price of the book.

—ROBERT G. TUTTLE JR., PhD
PROFESSOR OF WORLD CHRISTIANITY
ASBURY THEOLOGICAL SEMINARY

Becoming a Christ-follower is the first step in a new life. Becoming more like Christ (and becoming more like the persons we were born to be and now yearn to be) necessarily involves steps taken through prayer. *Nine Prayers of Promise* will help many believers to navigate the next steps in their Christian adventure.

—GEORGE G. HUNTER
DISTINGUISHED PROFESSOR OF
EVANGELISM AND CHURCH GROWTH
ASBURY THEOLOGICAL SEMINARY

Tim Westrom, following the example of Jesus, sets before us a simple and yet profound image that reveals God's design for transforming our lives "from one degree of glory to another." These nine prayers open the channels of the human heart to the flow of the Holy Spirit's sanctifying work, making us what we are meant to be—more like Jesus!

—RON CRANDALL
DEAN OF E. STANLEY JONES SCHOOL OF
WORLD MISSIONS AND EVANGELISM
SUNDO KIM PROFESSOR OF EVANGELISM AND
PRACTICAL THEOLOGY
ASBURY THEOLOGICAL SEMINARY

Tim Westrom has captured the heart of God in this book. It is a wonderful look at what happens when people are able to accept the love of God in their everyday living.

—Pastor Junius Lewis
Greater Love Family Outreach
Morgantown, West Virginia

Many today are searching for a spiritual reality that satisfies. Tim Westróm has outlined a pathway for a deeper relationship with God. The journey to discover the fruit of the Spirit in the life and ministry of Jesus Christ presents both a model and a challenge. May a multitude of readers take Tim's message to heart.

—Stephen E. Abe
District Executive Minister
West Marva District, Church of the Brethren

There are two things that make this book incredibly powerful. First, Tim Westrom knows firsthand what he writes about; his life illustrates the message of this book. Second, Tim tells the stories of Jesus so compellingly that as you read these pages your own love for Jesus will deepen, and you will want to join him on the path of prayer into the fruit of the Spirit.

—Reg Johnson, PhD
Roy and Wezzie Anderson
Chair of Prayer and Spiritual Formation
Dean of the School of Theology and Formation
Asbury Theological Seminary

TIM WESTROM

CREATION
HOUSE
A STRANG COMPANY

NINE PRAYERS OF PROMISE by Tim Westrom
Published by Creation House
A Strang Company
600 Rinehart Road
Lake Mary, Florida 32746
www.creationhouse.com

Unless otherwise noted, all Scripture quotations are from the New King James Version of the Bible. Copyright © 1979, 1980, 1982 by Thomas Nelson, Inc., publishers. Used by permission.

Scripture quotations marked NIV are from the Holy Bible, New International Version. Copyright © 1973, 1978, 1984, International Bible Society. Used by permission.

Scripture quotations marked CEV are from the Contemporary English Version, copyright © 1995 by the American Bible Society. Used by permission.

Cover design by Terry Clifton

Library of Congress Control Number: 2006926813
International Standard Book Number: 1-59979-051-3

First Edition

06 07 08 09 10 — 987654321
Printed in the United States of America

This book is dedicated to my wife, Rebecca Dawn Westrom. Your heart for Jesus is so beautiful. It has led me to fullness. I love you more than you will ever know.

Contents

Foreword

W E NEED HELP. I recently read a couple of articles that give a frightening synopsis of our culture. One referred to our time as an "age of rage." Apparently one in seven of us are ready, at any point, to explode in an act of violence. Another article, based on an Associated Press survey, called us an "impatient nation." Our blood boils after just five minutes of being on hold when we make a telephone call. We hate to go to the Department of Motor Vehicles because of the wait, but the number one place we hate to wait is the checkout line in the grocery store. The survey indicated that the cashier had better watch out if we have to wait more than fifteen minutes.

What will it take for love to survive in such a graceless age?

In *Nine Prayers of Promise*, Tim Westrom gives us the answer to this question. Love survives, no thrives, through people just like us who follow Jesus and allow the Holy Spirit to fill us and transform our character by His fruit.

Tim has grasped a truth that I believe has the potential to rock the world! Jesus didn't minister out of His own supernatural power. Remember, He emptied Himself of what was rightfully His

(Phil. 2). Jesus relied on the power of the Holy Spirit for His entire supernatural ministry. This is so important because He made it clear that we have access to that same power. That is why He could promise us that we, His followers, would do even greater things.

This book beckons us to live out this great potential. It weaves together Paul's powerful description of the fruit of the Spirit in Galatians 5 with engaging stories from Christ's ministry. And it echoes, page after page, with the spiritual call to let the Spirit of Christ fully transform each of us with ever increasing glory into the image of Jesus (2 Cor. 3:18).

You could read this book in one sitting; and you probably will want to. But I encourage you to savor it. Let it serve as a catalyst to an even greater experience. This book can take you right into the ministry of Jesus. Engage Him as He so beautifully displays love, joy, peace, patience, kindness, goodness, faithfulness, gentleness, and self-control. And as you lose yourself in the wonder of who He is, give His Spirit access to your spirit. As Paul says in Ephesians 4:18, "Let the Spirit fill your life" (CEV). *This* is the answer we need in such a graceless age.

—RICH STEVENSON
DIRECTOR, THE EXPANSION NETWORK
AUTHOR, *SECRETS OF THE SPIRITUAL LIFE* AND
A VOICE FROM HOME

Introduction

When He, the Spirit of truth, has come, He will guide you into all truth; for He will not speak on His own authority, but whatever He hears He will speak; and He will tell you things to come. He will glorify Me, for He will take of what is Mine and declare it to you. All things that the Father has are Mine. Therefore I said that He will take of Mine and declare it to you.

—JOHN 16:13–15

Have you ever wondered why the Holy Spirit is called "holy"? We know that the Father, the Son, and the Holy Spirit are all completely holy. Why then do we refer to the Spirit as the Holy Spirit? It is because of what He accomplishes in our lives, or what some would call His office. The Holy Spirit makes us holy. Sanctification—making us more like Jesus—is the Holy Spirit's enterprise.

Recently I received one of the most profound revelations of my spiritual life. While I was reflecting on the writings of Paul the Apostle, I came across one of the names he used for the Holy Spirit. It is the "Spirit of Jesus Christ," found in Philippians 1:19. (Similar names are given in Romans 8:9 and Galatians 4:6.) At that moment, Jesus' words in John 16 became clear to me. The desire of the Holy Spirit is to mold us into the image of the Son of God. Paul's name for the Spirit of God clarifies the vision of the Holy Spirit for our lives.

We don't have to wonder what the Holy Spirit is trying to do. His desire is that we worship the Father by being imitators of His Son. The Holy Spirit is eager to replicate the beauty of Christ in our lives, and this is His will for all men and women. We are not to supplant the supremacy of Christ by thinking of ourselves more highly than we ought; instead, as children of the King, we are to serve Him wholeheartedly. We cannot worship God as we should without the person of the Holy Spirit.

True worship happens in the midst of life, and it is impossible without the transforming presence of God. Worship is more than singing a song, lifting our hands, or bowing on our knees. Worship has to do with being, and it happens in the very core of who we are. Worship flowed continually from the heart of Christ. The Holy Spirit has the power to make us like Christ, and this is what He longs to do. Jesus is the epitome of holiness, and it is the desire of the Holy Spirit to make us like Him.

God confirmed this truth in my life as I began to study the fruit of the Spirit. Galatians 5:22 says "the fruit of the Spirit is love, joy, peace, patience, kindness, goodness, faithfulness, gentleness and self-control" (NIV). As I reflected on this list, I was drawn to the Gospels and their beautiful record of the life of Jesus, the perfect example of the fruit of the Spirit. The heart behind Jesus' character is the Spirit's desire for all Christians. Jesus wants the desires of our hearts to become like His.

Notice that the Bible talks about the fruit of the Spirit and not the fruits. This is very significant because the Holy Spirit wants those who trust in Jesus Christ to exhibit all the fruit not just individual fruits. For example, it is not enough to be gentle; we must also be loving. We cannot be faithful or good without being kind. There is no such thing as joy apart from peace, and self-control must include patience.

It is impossible to produce the fruit of the Spirit without the supernatural work of God. Through faith and trust in Jesus Christ, we receive the power of the Holy Spirit to lead holy lives, and this is the only way to bring God pleasure. To this end, I pray that the

Holy Spirit will use this book to immerse us in the true story of Jesus and draw us deeper into the desire of the Holy Spirit.

As we peer into the heart behind the fruit of the Spirit, we will discover the face of Jesus Christ—the King of kings and Lord of lords. Let us pray that the Holy Spirit of promise (Eph. 1:13) will open our eyes to the beauty of the Savior's life as it is shown in the Gospels. Oh the joy of catching even a glimpse of His life as it overflows from the sacred pages! My prayer is that we will see new, fresh glimmers of the Savior's goodness.

This is a book about the ministry of the Holy Spirit and His desire to take us from "glory to glory" (2 Cor. 3:7–18). Life is often hard, but Jesus has not left us alone. Real power is available to every believer through the truth of the cross. God's grace is bursting with joy and hope, and the Holy Spirit is eager to fulfill His promises. The toughest times and the biggest problems fade away in the light of the Son.

The Holy Spirit's deepest longing is for us to be captivated by the beauty of the Lord. It is impossible to see Jesus for who He really is and not be forever changed. May the pages that follow draw us to Jesus and a fuller experience with each fruit of the Spirit as we seek Him through the pathway of prayer.

Chapter 1

The Fruit of Love

Greater love has no one than this, than to lay down one's life for his friends.

—JOHN 15:13

SCRIPTURE: MATTHEW 27:27–56

The Savior is surrounded by hostile Roman soldiers. As they hem Him in, they strip away His outer garments and put a scarlet robe on Him, not for warmth on this early morning but to humiliate Him. One soldier parts the bullying circle for a moment to make a crown of thorns and quickly returns to adorn Jesus with this symbol of pain. Another soldier grabs a reed and places it in Jesus' hand. These are the tokens they deem fitting for this King.

Jesus doesn't lash out or use the reed as a weapon; instead He weeps inside as He beholds the emptiness of those around Him. He grieves deeply with the realization that these men have no idea He has come from heaven to die for their sins.

Now the soldiers begin to bow down before Him and shout, "Hail, King of the Jews!" As they continue this cynical ceremony they spit on Him and hurl insults at Him. One prideful young man takes the reed from Jesus' hand and strikes Him on the head. Others among the merciless tormenters take a turn, passing the

1

makeshift club among themselves. Then, instead of beating Jesus to death, the soldiers remove the blood-soiled scarlet robe from Him and put His own clothes on Him.

The King is hurt, dizzy from the blows, but He is strong. Not once does He curse these men even though He created them and has the power to take their lives. Instead He remembers who they were created to be. There seems to be no resemblance between His plan for them and the path they have chosen. As He wipes the blood from His chin and forehead, He prays that their eyes would be opened. He will gladly die in their place, if only they will turn to the truth. Jesus' prayers intensify in mercy as the soldiers lead Him to Calvary, the place of execution.

When they arrive at Calvary, the soldiers offer Jesus a drink. He cautiously takes a sip from the worn wooden cup only to realize that it is a narcotic meant to ease His obvious pain. He knows that this may hinder His final moments of prayer, and He spits it out. He will need a sound mind as He offers Himself for sinful mankind in this God-ordained event that is the hinge of all history. He knows why He is here. You can see it in His face, even if every other face in the mob is filled with mockery and anger. In His face, you see love.

The soldiers strip Jesus of His garments once again and then nail His arms and feet to the wooden cross. They show no remorse as they complete Pilate's decree. By now it is 9 AM and the streets are filled with onlookers. Some look at Him in pity and others shake their fists in scorn. A soldier comes with a decree to place a sign at the top of the cross: "THIS IS JESUS KING OF THE JEWS."

If only they knew the significance and irony of those words, Jesus thinks, as He speaks to the Father on their behalf. As His cross is lifted up the onlookers decide to take a seat and watch Him die. Although He has not been left alone since the previous night, Jesus is still in complete communion with His Father.

Those who pass by blaspheme Him, shaking their heads in disgust. The scribes and Pharisees revile Him in His pain and join in the onslaught of insult. And two thieves who are crucified alongside Jesus, one on His left and the other on His right, also lash out against Him.

As noon approaches the skies become mysteriously dark, and the crowd gathered beneath the cross is filled with wonder. For three hours Jesus suffers in darkness. At 3 PM He cries out, "My God, My God, why have you forsaken me?" Some people think that He is calling out for the prophet Elijah to save Him. Little do they know that His blood is providing salvation for all people, including Elijah.

The reality of the moment can be seen in Jesus' eyes. For the first time in His life He feels the poison of sin. It is not His own; He is shouldering the weight of the sins of the world and taking it upon Himself. For the first time in His life He takes a breath apart from the Father. Jesus cries out again with a loud voice and gives up His spirit, offering His life as an atoning sacrifice for our sins.

Look into the eyes of Christ as He suffers and dies at Calvary. Consider the heart behind the cross. Listen as Jesus whispers, "I am doing this for you." Experience the depths of His love at the foot of the cross. On that dreary wooden cross, Jesus—surrounded by His enemies—loves them and gives His life for them. There is no greater love! The Bible says, "God demonstrates His own love toward us, in that while we were still sinners, Christ died for us." (Romans 5:8)

Love made the cross possible. What else could have inspired Jesus to take that torment? Jesus faced more cruelty, hatred, and pain than any other person in history, as Isaiah 53 foretold. And He did it willingly because of His deep love for His Father and His deep love for us!

Christ is our model, and love is the motivating force that led Him to the cross so we may have life. The Holy Spirit plants the seed of Christ's love in us. It is the first fruit of the Holy Spirit and the chief cornerstone of all that follow. Jesus has promised to pour His love into the hearts of those who are thirsty for Him. Romans 5:5 says, "The love of God has been poured out in our hearts by the Holy Spirit who was given to us."

God has shown us mercy through the tremendous love of Christ. We can express no greater act of gratitude than to let Him fill us with that same love. God is love, and love is the beginning—and essence—of all that comes from Him. The Bible says, "He who abides in love abides in God, and God in him" (1 John 4:16). Finding the fullness of God's love within should always be at the center of our prayers. We must abide in the love of God.

Holy Father God, thank You for Your Son Jesus! Thank You for the example of love that I find in His heart! Thank You for the portrait of love that I see in the self-giving Christ. Send Your Holy Spirit. Fill me afresh with Your holy presence, so I may love like You. Let Your fruit be magnified in my life. I ask this in the loving name of Jesus. Amen.

Chapter 2

The Fruit of Joy

Therefore we also, since we are surrounded by so great a cloud of witnesses, let us lay aside every weight, and the sin which so easily ensnares us, and let us run with endurance the race that is set before us, looking unto Jesus, the author and finisher of our faith, who for the joy set before Him endured the cross, despising the shame, and has sat down at the right hand of the throne of God.

—HEBREWS 12:1-2

SCRIPTURE: JOHN 20:11-18

It is early Sunday morning, and Mary is tired. She is in shock from Jesus' death, and she has not been able to sleep since His crucifixion on Friday. The cool morning breeze blows through her hair as she reflects on the only real father figure she has ever known. She ponders the forgiving words He spoke over her life, and the peace that flooded her soul when He taught from the Scriptures.

Tears begin to well from Mary's eyes as she remembers how He set her free from the cruel oppression of the devil. In this time of misery the pain of her past seems so close. She remembers the weight of anxiety, the punishing voices, and the daily pain. She recalls how it felt to experience true peace for the first time. These past few days have been the most sorrowful she has ever known.

Peter and John have just left the tomb site in disbelief. Mary begins to weep as she embraces her hopeless thoughts. She stoops down, peers into the tomb, and is astonished to see two angels. One is sitting at the head and the other at the foot of the place where Jesus' body had been placed. Her jaw drops in amazement as the angels ask her, "Woman, why are you weeping?"

"Because they have taken away my Lord," she mourns, "and I do not know where they have laid Him."

Mary turns around and sees a man she does not recognize. "Woman, why are you weeping?" he asks her. "Whom are you seeking?"

This must be the gardener, she thinks. "Sir," she petitions him, "if you have carried Him away, tell me where you have laid Him, and I will take Him away."

The joy in His heart and the expression in His voice give Him away as He exclaims, "Mary!"

There is no doubt in her mind about the identity of this joyous presence in the garden. "Teacher!" she exults, as a river of joy begins to flow from her heart. At that moment Mary thought about her favorite parable of the Prodigal Son, and reached for the hands of her Lord. What started as the most miserable day of her life has been transformed in His presence.

Jesus tells Mary, "Do not cling to Me, for I have not yet ascended to My Father and Your Father, and to My God and your God." After hearing this, she runs back down the dusty road to tell the disciples that Jesus is alive. She knows she will never be the same.

"I am ascending to My Father and your Father, and to My God and your God." Can you feel the joy emanating from these words of Jesus? He has conquered sin and death, and He knows that all people can now receive the Father's love through what has transpired on the cross. What joy Jesus must feel as He visits with His followers the next forty days! As He looks upon them, He knows

6

that the judgment for their sins has been paid. How long He has passionately waited for this day to come!

ᕙ

Nothing gives God greater joy than the restoration of one of His lost children. Luke 15:20–24 paints a picture of our heavenly Father as a God of joy when the prodigal son leaves his life of sin and returns home. In the same chapter the parable of the lost sheep quotes the words of the Good Shepherd,

> Rejoice with me, for I have found my sheep which was lost! I say to you that likewise there will be more joy in heaven over one sinner who repents than over ninety-nine just persons who need no repentance.
>
> —LUKE 15:6–7

Again, Luke 15 records the parable of the lost coin. God reveals in verse 10 that "there is joy in the presence of the angels of God over one sinner who repents." Our God is a God of joy, and that joy is directly related to the salvation and freedom of His children.

Is it any wonder that joy is a fruit of the Spirit? God expresses joy because we return to Him in faith and repentance, and we have joy because He is alive and well. The resurrection is the foundation of our joy. Romans 8:11 says:

> But if the Spirit of Him who raised Jesus from the dead dwells in you, He who raised Christ from the dead will also give life to your mortal bodies through His Spirit who dwells in you.

The Holy Spirit raised Jesus from the grave, and it is the same Spirit who produces the fruit of joy in our hearts.

In John 16:16 Jesus tells His disciples that although He was going away, they would see Him again. He precedes this declaration of hope by promising to send the Holy Spirit to be their helper through hard times (John 16:1–7). In verse 22 He says,

"Therefore you now have sorrow; but I will see you again and your heart will rejoice, and your joy no one will take from you." Although we do not necessarily rejoice for all things, we can rejoice in all things. The Holy Spirit gives us joy to carry us through our difficulties. He reminds us that Jesus is alive, and that He cares for us. Just as Mary's sorrow was turned to joy by the revelation of the resurrection, we too can experience joy through the fact that Jesus is alive and with us through the Person of His Spirit (John 20:20). The ministry of the Holy Spirit will prepare us to stand before Jesus when this life fades. He alone can make us ready for that day and prepare us for heaven by making us holy.

Because Jesus' blood was poured out for our sins, we can receive the Holy Spirit and the fruit of joy. The Bible also gives us reason to celebrate when it declares that Jesus was the "firstfruits" of those who have placed their lives in His hands and will be raised from the dead when He comes again (1 Cor. 15:20–23). Our bodies will be restored to life and transformed into incorruptible, glorious, and powerful spiritual bodies. (See 1 Corinthians 15:35–58.) God will give us resurrection life by the power of the Holy Spirit.

Our God has plans that are above and beyond our understanding. It is His desire to make us holy, fill us with joy, and raise our bodies incorruptible on the final day. Is it any wonder that He wants us to be filled with the power of the Holy Spirit? If nothing brings God greater joy than the salvation of His people, Christ's words in Acts 1:8 hold special significance for all believers. In His final words before He ascended to the right hand of the Father, Jesus said:

> But you shall receive power when the Holy Spirit has come upon you; and you shall be witnesses to Me in Jerusalem, and in all Judea and Samaria, and to the end of the earth.

The Spirit-filled life has always been centered on evangelism because God's passion is poured out in our hearts by His abounding presence. Nothing gives God joy like the sinner who comes home.

And nothing can elevate our souls like the presence of the Holy Spirit as He draws us into God's plans and purposes for the world.

Precious Lord Jesus, thank You for reconciling me to the Father! Thank You for sending the Holy Spirit so I might receive power to be free from sin, to live out the abundant life of joy (John 10:10), and to be Your witness! Please cultivate the fruit of joy in my heart, and give me the strength to be an agent of joy for Your kingdom. Thank You that the Holy Spirit gives power to live joyously, even in the hard times (James 1:2). Thank You for the anointing of joy that we find in Your presence, Lord God (Heb. 1:9)! Please keep me in Your loving arms of joy, and please keep me from quenching the Spirit's fire in my heart (1 Thess. 5:16–19). You are the God of resurrection power (1 Pet. 3:18)! In Jesus' mighty and wonderful name. Amen.

Chapter 3

The Fruit of Peace

These things I have spoken to you, that in Me you may have peace. In the world you will have tribulation; but be of good cheer, I have overcome the world.

—JOHN 16:33

SCRIPTURE: MATTHEW 8:23–27; MARK 4:35–41

Another long day has come to an end. As the sun falls behind the hills, Jesus and His disciples board a rickety old fishing boat, and set out for the east side of the Sea of Galilee. With wonder and astonishment, the disciples recount the glorious miracles they have just seen, but an exhausted Jesus heads for the stern of the ship. Carrying the burden of the masses and healing the multitudes has taken its toll on the Master. He makes himself comfortable, pauses in silent prayer, and drifts off to sleep.

It is now dark, and thick, gray clouds suddenly sweep across the sky, hiding the stars. As the wind rips across the sea and tosses the boat with reckless abandon, the memory-filled conversation of the disciples comes to an abrupt halt. The group looks to Peter, James, and John—the fishermen of the group—for help, but they find none. In all their years on the sea they

11

have never encountered a storm like this. Fear and anxiety grip them as the boat begins to take on water. With panic-stricken hearts, they rush to Jesus, who is still sleeping.

As another wave crashes into the boat, they stumble to their knees and cry out, "Lord save us! We are perishing!"

Awakened by their desperate plea, Jesus replies, "Why are you fearful, O you of little faith?" Rising to His feet, He rebukes the wind and the sea with the simple words, "Peace, be still!"

The disciples are amazed as a great calm immediately replaces the violent storm. These men are familiar with the Psalms and their testimony that God alone can tame the great deep. (See Psalms 74:13–15, 89:9, 107:23–31.) They look at each other in amazement and ask, "Who can this be, that even the wind and the sea obey Him!" What was once a raging sea is now a picture of tranquility. This is a day the disciples will never forget.

Are the storms of life pummeling your ship of faith? Are clouds of anxiety blocking your view of the Father? Is fear crippling your future? Jesus is willing and able to deliver you from chaos and torment. In the words of 1 Corinthians 7:15, "God has called us to peace." He has not left us as orphans in this fallen world. Jesus has promised:

> These things I have spoken to you while being present with you. But the Helper, the Holy Spirit, whom the Father will send in My name, He will teach you all things, and bring to your remembrance all things that I said to you. Peace I leave with you, My peace I give to you; not as the world gives do I give to you. Let not your heart be troubled, neither let it be afraid.
>
> —JOHN 14:25–27

Jesus has given us the Holy Spirit so we can live in peace. In Colossians 3:15 the apostle Paul instructs us to let "the peace of God rule" in our hearts. The Holy Spirit is that peace. John the Baptist prophesied that Jesus would baptize us with the Holy Spirit (Mark 1:8). The baptism of the Holy Spirit is a supernatural work of grace that we experience as we surrender ourselves to God. Jesus promised that He would leave us His peace, and this happens when we accept Him as Lord, and surrender our all to His life-giving Spirit.

The Bible says that both the Holy Spirit and Jesus are Comforters (John 14:16) and we also know that Jesus "is our peace" (Eph. 2:14). The beauty of the baptism of the Holy Spirit is that we can now experience comfort from within. Jesus told the disciples that it was to their advantage for Him to ascend into heaven, so the Comforter could not only be with them but also within them (John 16:7). The Holy Spirit can now take residence in our hearts because of what Jesus did on the cross.

As a result of this, we can be instruments of God's peace and power in the world. Despite our human weakness and fragility, we can be of great use to God, because of His presence within us. Our communities need this ministry of peace and comfort so desperately. Jesus hasn't given us this gift to keep to ourselves. It is His plan that we be ambassadors of His peace in the world. Praise God for the promised ministry of the Comforter!

Jesus Christ is the Prince of Peace, and He has made it possible for us to have peace as we live in our fallen world. Romans 5:1 says, "Therefore, having been justified by faith, we have peace with God through our Lord Jesus Christ." By "the blood of His cross" we find peace with God (Col. 1:20). There is no true peace apart from faith and trust in Jesus Christ. Our Lord was not insensitive when He slept in the stern of the boat while the disciples were struck with fear. He simply trusted the faithfulness of His Father. In the same way we can have peace within by trusting Jesus as our Lord.

Peace is a supernatural work of God, and it is a hallmark of the Spirit-filled life. God desires that every Christian live in the abundance of this perfect rest. The Holy Spirit wants to make our hearts into homes of peace. He desires to bring forth the fruit of peace in us.

Psalm 139:7–10 says:

> Where can I go from Your Spirit? Or where can I flee
> from Your presence? If I ascend into heaven, You are
> there; If I make my bed in hell, behold, You are there. If
> I take the wings of the morning, And dwell in the utter-
> most parts of the sea, Even there Your hand shall lead
> me, And Your right hand shall hold me.

We have no greater comfort than the assurance that God is
not only near us, but also within us. Perfect peace comes from
knowing that the Spirit of God is always with us. There is no
greater authority than our loving God, and there is nothing
that He cannot do. The love of our awesome God is unstop-
pable, and there is nothing that He does not know. No evil can
overtake Him or even surprise Him. His perfect will cannot be
thwarted. We can rest in all surpassing peace, even when the
waves of uncertainty threaten our journey, because we serve the
one and only God almighty.

*God of love and peace (2 Cor. 13:11), come and transform
me. Make my heart a home for Your peace. Help me to cast
my anxieties away as I come to you in prayer (Phil. 4:6–7).
Flood my heart with the Person of Your Holy Spirit. Calm
the raging seas that threaten me, and help me to have the
faith You desire. Empower me, Lord, to be an ambassador
of the peace of Your kingdom in this world. Thank You for
the love I find in Your ministry of peace. In the name of
Jesus Christ—the Prince of Peace—I pray. Amen.*

Chapter 4

The Fruit of Patience

**Let patience have its perfect work, that you may
be perfect and complete, lacking nothing.**
—JAMES 1:4

SCRIPTURE: LUKE 2:39–52

The sun is setting, and Joseph begins to set up camp. As Mary
approaches him, anxiety is written on her countenance. She ner-
vously tells him that she cannot find Jesus anywhere. She has
checked with all of the family, and no one has seen Him since they
left Jerusalem. "We must have left Him there!" she exclaims.

"Don't worry, Mary," Joseph replies. "He's twelve years old and
you know how bright He is. We'll find Him. He'll be OK."

Mary and Joseph return to Jerusalem, and after three days,
they still cannot find Jesus. Joseph's heart sinks in despair as he
tells Mary, "I just don't know where else to look."

With a gleam in her eye, Mary replies, "I know, He must be
in the temple!" They rush down the street and up the steps to
the temple entrance. There He is, surrounded by the teachers. As
soon as Joseph sees Jesus he begins to stride toward Him. Mary,
however, reaches out and stops her husband.

Her eyes are locked on Jesus as He stands in the center of Israel's

15

religious leaders and teaches from the Law and the prophets. Every word He speaks is filled with wisdom and compassion.

Joseph's jaw drops in amazement as the teachers ask Jesus about His interpretation of various scriptures. He and Mary are dumbfounded as Jesus asks the leaders questions that prove His interpretation is true. "Where has He learned these wonderful things?" Joseph whispers to Mary.

As they watch Jesus, His eyes meet theirs. He smiles and leaves the discussion to hug His parents. Mary asks, "Son, why have you done this to us? Look, Your father and I have sought You anxiously."

Jesus replies with a gentle, searching question, "Why did you seek Me? Did you not know that I must be about my Father's business?"

Joseph and Mary look at Jesus with confusion. What does He mean by His Father's business?

Jesus wants so much for Joseph and Mary to understand His response, but He recognizes that He must be patient with them. He knows that He is God in human form, conceived by the Holy Spirit and born of the virgin Mary. Yet, it is His heavenly Father's will that He honor Mary and Joseph.

He turns and waves good-bye to the teachers and follows His earthly parents out of the temple. A few of them come to Joseph and ask him where this child had received such extraordinary teaching. "It is a gift from God," Joseph replies as he places his hand on Jesus' shoulder.

Jesus returns to Nazareth and continues to exercise patience as He waits for the proper time to begin His ministry. He could demonstrate His spiritual authority in a more dramatic way, but He honors His heavenly Father by obeying the Scriptures. He lives according to the Father's perfect plan.

Can you see the patience of Christ in His subjection to His parents? They did not understand that He was to be about His Father's business, but He was patient.

Do you see His patience as He waited for the Father's timing to enter His kingdom ministry? He knew the Scriptures, and He often quoted the Psalms and Isaiah. He was no stranger to Psalm 22 and other prophecies that foretold His death. Yet He was patient. He understood that the Father's will is perfect, and He submitted to His plan. The relationship within the Trinity is one of complete trust and unity.

Jesus lived a life of patience. His relationship with His disciples reveals a heart of patience and love. Even when they denied Him and deserted Him, He remained patient with them. He knew they needed the ministry of the Holy Spirit, and He eagerly waited for the day of Pentecost when they would be empowered.

His patience continues today as He waits for the lost to turn to Him. The apostle Peter said:

> The Lord is not slow in keeping his promise, as some understand slowness. He is patient with you, not wanting anyone to perish, but everyone to come to repentance. But the day of the Lord will come like a thief. The heavens will disappear with a roar; the elements will be destroyed by fire, and the earth and everything in it will be laid bare.
>
> —2 PETER 3:9–10, NIV

The Lord Jesus wants to come for His bride the church, but He is patiently waiting so the Holy Spirit can bring more people into the fold. Christ is lovingly and patiently stalling for the sake of the lost. He desires that more people will come and receive the gift of grace He provided by His death on the cross. How He wishes all men and women would respond to the Holy Spirit's call by repenting and entering the family of God!

The Holy Spirit desires that we exercise the fruit of patience. Just as Jesus waited patiently for the day of salvation to be revealed, we also must wait for the leading of the Holy Spirit in our lives. It takes patience to be led by the Spirit. Patience is required in the life of faith, and it is needed to live a life pleasing to God. This holy endurance is the work of the Holy Spirit.

Father in heaven, You are the God of patience and comfort (Rom. 15.5)! Help me to live in holy endurance. Patience is found in You and You alone. Please give me the grace to follow in Your footsteps of patience. I want to live out this love that never gives up. Let all of humanity know the love that is behind Your patience and in Your precious blood, Lord Jesus! Thank You for the work of the Holy Spirit. In Jesus' powerful and patient name I pray. Amen.

Chapter 5

The Fruit of Kindness

And be kind to one another, tenderhearted, forgiving one another, even as God in Christ forgave you.

—EPHESIANS 4:32

SCRIPTURE: LUKE 22:47–53; JOHN 18:1–12

It seems like any other night. The stars are shining, and the wind is blowing gently through the olive trees. The disciples are resting in the comfort of the familiar place of prayer. All seems well to the untrained eye. But take a closer look at the face of Jesus. What do you see?

Jesus knows that this night is like none other. He has just labored in prayer in Gethsemane, the garden of the oil press, and He has felt the weight of the Father's will for Him to suffer on the cross. He can see the armies of darkness assembling in the spirit world, and He knows this will be the night He faces the evil one head-on.

Satan has already entered Judas, who is leading a group of soldiers and officials to take Him captive. Little does Judas know that everything is going according to God's plan. The Father's love story is unfolding, and God the Son will play the leading part.

19

Suddenly, the quietness of the garden is interrupted. Can you hear the trudging footsteps and the muffled voices? A great commotion is stirring near the gate, and the disciples hurry to their feet. *Who is it? Should we hide?* they wonder.

But Jesus is a picture of peace and strength. "Whom are you seeking?" He calls out in the cool night air.

Approaching in the darkness is the familiar form of Judas, followed by an angry mob armed with swords and clubs. Several men jeer, "Jesus of Nazareth."

Jesus calmly replies, "I am He."

The whole mass of people fall to the ground in fear. They have heard of Jesus' miracles and power, and now they look among themselves, wondering who will be courageous enough to attempt His arrest. No one is willing to try.

Jesus calls out again with the kindest voice they have ever heard. "Whom are you seeking?" You can feel the invitation to come closer.

"Jesus of Nazareth," the soldiers reply weakly. They regroup as Judas begins his betrayal march to Jesus. He has told them that he will reveal the identity of Jesus by kissing Him on the cheek.

Jesus is no stranger to the schemes of the serpent. He has seen his slithering nature in the life of Judas. "Judas," Jesus asked, "are you betraying the Son of Man with a kiss?"

The mob's brief expression of fear has reverted to anger. As the disciples notice this, they cry out to Jesus, "Lord shall we strike with the sword?"

Before Jesus can answer, Peter attacks the most threatening man in the group, cutting off his ear. However, Jesus takes control of the chaos and commands His disciples, "No more of this."

No more of this? The disciples are amazed. Doesn't Jesus know that these men have come to kill Him?

The injured man—Malchus—has had nothing but hatred for Jesus up to this point. Now, however, he is bleeding profusely, and the fear of death grips him as he falls to his knees. As he weeps in pain, he suddenly feels the purest sensation he has ever known. Jesus is touching the place where his ear had been, and all his pain is leaving. He runs his hand across the side of his face and discovers that his ear has been completely restored. As he looks up, he gazes into a face that radiates the beauty of kindness.

Jesus turns to Peter and tells him to put his sword away. He knows that He could call on the Father and more than twelve legions of angels would be dispatched to His rescue (Matt. 26:53). Instead, He allows the angry mob to take Him to the high priest and on to Pilate. He willingly goes to be tried and then crucified so He can give eternal life to all who will call on His name. He goes to fulfill the Father's plan so Peter and Malchus and anyone who trusts in Him can receive His kindness.

Did Malchus find salvation that night long ago? Did this servant of the high priest change allegiance in the moment he received Jesus' healing touch? If anything could transform his callous heart, it was the kindness of Jesus. It is hard to imagine heaven without Malchus. I believe the kindness of the Son of Man brought conviction and change to his heart forever.

Romans 2:4 says that God's kindness leads us to repentance. We also know that the Holy Spirit convicts the world of sin, righteousness, and judgment (John 16:8–11). Isn't it amazing how the Holy Spirit leads us to repentance by revealing the overpowering kindness of God?

The kindness of Calvary convicts the world of sin, and the Holy Spirit desires to fill us with the kindness modeled there. This fruit of the Spirit is the answer to a hurting world. Nothing else can transform a bitter, angry heart.

Come Holy Spirit; fill me with the kindness of Christ. It was through Your kindness, Lord Jesus, that I found the refuge of repentance and the gift of grace. Thank You for that kindness. Do Your will in my life, Holy Spirit. Bring forth the fruit of kindness in my heart so others may know the mercy of God the Father. Let Jesus' kindness to Malchus be the model for my life. I ask this in the kind and compassionate name of Jesus. Amen.

Chapter 6

The Fruit of Goodness

For you were once darkness, but now you are light in the Lord. Walk as children of the light (for the fruit of the Spirit is in all goodness, righteousness, and truth), finding out what is acceptable to the Lord. And have no fellowship with the unfruitful works of darkness, but rather expose them.

—EPHESIANS 5:8–12

SCRIPTURE: MATTHEW 3:13–4:11

Jesus has just been baptized. The Holy Spirit has descended upon Him like a dove, and the Father has audibly confirmed His identity and commended Him before those gathered. This has warmed His heart, and Jesus is blessed as He thinks of His loving Father and His heavenly home. He is encouraged because the Spirit, with His abiding presence, has come down upon Him. It has been an amazing day, and Jesus knows that He is being prepared for His Father's will.

Jesus is then led by the Spirit into the wilderness to be tempted by the devil. This marks the beginning of a forty-day fast in which Jesus seeks closer fellowship with the Father and devotes Himself to prayer. After these days filled with the closest of communion with the Father, Jesus is extremely hungry.

It is then that Jesus notices He is not alone. There in the dark is the enemy of all that is good and holy. Jesus is not surprised by his arrival, for He knew that the enemy would strike at His most vulnerable point. Nor is Jesus afraid. Instead, He is confident and encouraged as the words of His Father echo among His thoughts. He senses the empowering of the Spirit who descended upon Him forty days earlier. Jesus is ready!

The old serpent, Satan, challenges Jesus, "If you are the Son of God, command that these stones become bread." The father of lies is attacking the identity of the Son of God, and Jesus is aware of his subtle ploy. Satan wants Him to take the glory He had held in heaven, to step out of the incarnation, and back into His completely divine position.

Jesus knows the consequences of such an action. If He gives up His humanness, He will forfeit His calling to save lost humanity. Jesus refuses to abuse the power of the Holy Spirit for His own gain. He rebukes Satan with the written word and replies, "It is written, 'Man shall not live by bread alone, but by every word that proceeds from the mouth of God.'"

Something within the serpent quivers as these words flow from the lips of the incarnate Son. But he does not give up! He takes Jesus into Jerusalem to the pinnacle of the temple, and once again attacks Him with doubt about His identity. He says:

> If you are the Son of God, throw Yourself down. For it is written: "He shall give His angels charge over you," and "In their hands they shall bear you up, Lest you dash your foot against a stone."
>
> —MATTHEW 4:6

This time the enemy has chosen to use the written word from Psalm 91:11–12 against the Son of Man; however, he understands nothing of holy inspiration. Jesus knows the true interpretation, as He stands upon the promises of God. The enemy is using the Word as it was never intended. He is quoting Scripture in an attempt to get Jesus outside of the Father's will. Satan is seductively trying to get Jesus to lay aside His servant heart for the glory this world has to offer. Jesus replies, "It is written again, 'You shall not tempt the Lord your God.'"

The adversary is filled with rage at the truth that emits so naturally from the heart of Jesus. He has tempted Jesus' commitment to the way of the cross (verse 3), as well as His trust and commitment to the Father (verse 6). Jesus has passed both tests with flying colors, displaying His humility, power, and obedience to the will of God! But the evil one has one more temptation—his favorite and the most alluring of all.

This time the devil takes Jesus to the top of a very high mountain. He shows Jesus all the kingdoms of the world and all their most extravagant treasures. Flashing every possible pleasure and every allurement the world has to offer, Satan holds nothing back. With an attitude of confidence the serpent says, "All these things I will give You if You will fall down and worship me."

Jesus looks squarely into the face of deceit and darkness and rails, "Away with you, Satan! For it is written, 'You shall worship the Lord your God, and Him only you shall serve.'"

Satan leaves in defeat. Jesus has faced the onslaught of the enemy and prevailed. As He rests in the comfort of the Spirit, the angels of God come and minister to Him.

Jesus' defeat of Satan in the wilderness temptations was the greatest revelation of goodness. The enemy had come with deception and doubt, trying to draw Jesus into the snare of sin. However, his efforts revealed the perfect holiness and glorious light that filled the soul of Jesus.

The Book of Hebrews comments on Jesus' experience with temptation:

> Therefore, in all things He had to be made like His brethren, that He might be a merciful and faithful High Priest in things pertaining to God, to make propitiation for the sins of the people. For in that He Himself has suffered, being tempted, He is able to aid those who are tempted.
>
> —HEBREWS 2:17–18

Jesus is no stranger to temptation. He faced more opposition from the enemy than anyone, and yet He never sinned. Even in the secret place of the wilderness, in complete solitude, Jesus remained faithful. This is the essence of the fruit of goodness! What is done in the secret place—behind closed doors—is the true test of goodness. Romans 2:4 teaches that we are not to "despise the riches of His goodness."

The Holy Spirit desires to remove all darkness, lust, and carnality from our hearts. He desperately wants us to die to the sinful nature that plagues humanity as a result of the fall in Genesis 3. The apostle Paul said:

> Walk in the Spirit, and you shall not fulfill the lust of the flesh. For the flesh lusts against the Spirit, and the Spirit against the flesh; and these are contrary to one another, so that you do not do the things that you wish.
>
> —GALATIANS 5:16–17

As we surrender ourselves to the Spirit of God, we will receive liberty from the desires of the flesh. The Holy Spirit will clean us up and fertilize the fruit of goodness within our hearts.

Jesus will draw near to us as we draw near to Him. He has not left us defenseless against the wiles of the devil, but He has given us real power through the Holy Spirit and in the Scriptures. When Jesus did battle with the enemy He used the Word of God. He knew it because it was written upon His heart. In Ephesians 6:10–17 Paul admonished all believers to put on the armor of God. Isn't it amazing that the only offensive weapon He provides is the "sword of the Spirit, which is the word of God" (Eph. 6.17)!

The devil tempted Jesus by quoting the Scriptures, but his interpretation had no authority because it was not of the Holy Spirit. Second Timothy 3:16 teaches that the Holy Spirit inspired the Word of God, and He alone can give us true understanding of it (1 Cor. 2:9–14). Second Peter 1:20–21 says, "No prophecy of Scripture is of any private interpretation, for prophecy never came by the will of man, but holy men of God spoke as they were moved by the Holy Spirit."

A quality of holy love must mark all biblical interpretation. As we prayerfully receive God's Word, the Holy Spirit applies it to our lives and leads us to freedom. The apostle Peter said:

> Since you have purified your souls in obeying the truth through the Spirit in sincere love of the brethren, love one another fervently with a pure heart, having been born again, not of corruptible seed but incorruptible, through the word of God which lives and abides forever.
>
> —1 PETER 1:22–23

We need the Holy Spirit's ministry of goodness because we are capable of no good thing apart from His grace. We need His power and purity to be poured out in our hearts so we can be free from our carnal nature and practice integrity and holiness instead. The Holy Spirit births the fruit of goodness, and it is tested in the flames of our private lives. Just as Jesus was victorious over temptation in the wilderness, we also can have victory over sin through the power of the Holy Spirit.

Holy Father God, I am hungry for the power of Your Spirit in my life. Please give me the grace to walk in the Spirit, so I won't give in to the desires of the flesh. Defeat the enemy's schemes of doubt and deception in my life and in those around me. Write Your Word upon my heart, and send Your Spirit to inspire my reading of the Bible. I pray that the Holy Spirit will teach me how to apply the Word of God in my daily life as I seek to take up "the sword of the Spirit" (Eph. 6.17). Lead me, Lord, in the path of the fruit of goodness. In the sinless name of Jesus I pray. Amen.

Chapter 7

The Fruit of Faithfulness

Now may the God of peace Himself sanctify you completely; and may your whole spirit, soul, and body be preserved blameless at the coming of our Lord Jesus Christ. He who calls you is faithful, who also will do it.

—1 THESSALONIANS 5:23-24

SCRIPTURE: JOHN 11:1-44

The disciples wonder what message could be important enough to interrupt Jesus' teaching. As they eavesdrop on the conversation between Jesus and the young messenger, they learn that Lazarus, the brother of Mary and Martha, is very sick and close to death.

This is all the disciples need to hear, for they know how much Jesus loves this family. They remember how Martha had opened her home to Him and prepared a delightful feast for their entire group. Mary had sat at Jesus' feet, drinking in every word He spoke (Luke 10:38–42). They also know how much Jesus cares for Martha and Lazarus. The disciples begin to prepare for the journey to Bethany because they know Jesus will want to go and help immediately.

Jesus turns to them and says, "This sickness is not unto death, but for the glory of God, that the Son of God may be glorified through it." And then the disciples marvel as the messenger returns alone in the direction from which he had come.

After continuing His ministry where they are for two more days, Jesus tells His disciples, "Our friend Lazarus sleeps, but I go that I may wake him up."

The disciples are puzzled and reply, "Lord if he sleeps he will get well." They do not know that Jesus is speaking of his death.

The Master turns to the group and declares, "Lazarus is dead. And I am glad for your sakes that I was not there, that you may believe. Nevertheless let us go to him." And so they head for Bethany.

When Jesus and the disciples arrive there, Lazarus has been in the tomb four days. As they approach the home of Mary, Martha, and Lazarus, they notice a large group that has gathered to mourn. Martha hears that Jesus is coming, and she runs to Him. She knew He would come; she just wishes He would have come sooner. Mary, however, stays in the house. She has never known Jesus to be unfaithful; He has always responded to her cries for help. Why didn't He come back with the messenger? she wonders.

As Martha greets Jesus, she says, "Lord if You had been here, my brother would not have died. But even now I know that whatever You ask of God, God will give You."

Jesus looks at her with compassion and replies, "Your brother will rise again."

Looking away with a tear in her eye, Martha responds, "I know that he will rise again in the resurrection at the last day."

Jesus says, "I am the resurrection and the life. He who believes in Me, though he may die, he shall live. And whoever lives and believes in Me shall never die. Do you believe this?"

"Yes, Lord," Martha replies. "I believe that You are the Christ, the Son of God, who is to come into the world."

At Jesus' request, Martha runs to Mary with the message that He is calling for her. Mary gets up from her weeping and hurries to Jesus. Those who are comforting her think she is going to the tomb to mourn, and they follow her. When Mary comes to Jesus, she finds Him waiting patiently. Falling down at His feet, she says, "Lord if You had been here, my brother would not have died."

Jesus sees Mary weeping, and He is visibly moved and deeply troubled in spirit. "Where have you laid him?" He asks. As Jesus follows the mourners to the burial place, He weeps. The crowd realizes how much Jesus loved Lazarus, and some of them begin to question why He did not come earlier to stop his death.

At the cave where Lazarus is buried, Jesus asks the people to roll away the heavy stone that seals the entrance. Martha tries to discourage this because of the stench that will be present after four days of decay. But the Lord insists, "Did I not say to you that if you would believe you would see the glory of God?"

As several men roll away the stone that seals Lazarus' tomb, Jesus looks into the sky and prays:

> Father, I thank You that You have heard Me. And I know that You always hear Me, but because of the people who are standing by I said this, that they may believe that You sent Me.
>
> —JOHN 11:41–42

And then, Jesus cries out, "Lazarus come forth!" At that moment the lifeless body of Lazarus is filled with vitality, and he comes out of the tomb, bound from head to foot in grave clothes. "Loose him, and let him go," Jesus tells the people.

Can you feel the overflowing joy of Mary and Martha as they help untie their brother? Can you sense their overwhelming gratitude to God as they embrace their once deceased brother? Do they have any question about the faithfulness of the Lord? Mary and Martha had questioned why Jesus did not come earlier, but now they once again trust the faithfulness of Jesus. They can fully rest in the fact that Jesus always responds to a sincere cry for help.

∾

Do you see the fruit of faithfulness displayed in Jesus' life? He is the essence of faithfulness and truth. Satan tried to destroy the faith of Mary and Martha with his lies, but Jesus said no! He demonstrated the power of the kingdom of God when He delivered Lazarus from death, Satan's most powerful weapon. Second Thessalonians 3:3 says, "The Lord is faithful, who will establish you strong and guard you from the evil one."

The Lord is faithful to keep all His promises (Heb. 10:23). In 1 John 1:9 we read, "If we confess our sins, He is faithful and just to forgive us our sins and to cleanse us from all unrighteousness." First Corinthians 1:8 reminds us that we, through Christ, will be blameless on the day when He comes to judge the earth. He has provided victory over temptation and sin (1 Cor. 10:13).

We can trust in God's faithfulness regardless of any obstacle we face. He has provided power in the Person of the Holy Spirit! He has not left us as orphans. Jesus has promised the Holy Spirit, and He is faithful. He said:

> "If anyone thirsts, let him come to Me and drink. He who believes in Me, as the Scripture has said, out of his heart will flow rivers of living water." But this He spoke concerning the Spirit, whom those believing in Him would receive; for the Holy Spirit was not yet given, because Jesus was not yet glorified.
>
> —JOHN 7:37–39

This promise was first fulfilled on the Day of Pentecost when His followers received the power of the Holy Spirit in the upper room in Jerusalem (Acts 2:1–4). Previously fragile and inconsistent, the believers received the power and freedom to become what God created them to be. Peter preached and three thousand people experienced saving faith. Although Peter didn't become perfect in an instant, he was given the strength to overcome his sinful flesh. The Holy Spirit enabled him to live a life that pleases God.

It is impossible to live a holy life without the ministry of the Holy Spirit. Christ has promised us the Comforter if we will come to Him, thirsting for His holiness. We can rest in the faithful character of Christ, who gives us power to be faithful to the end (Heb. 3:14). Mary and Martha learned to trust in His faithfulness, and so must we!

> *Blessed Trinity of God, great is Your faithfulness (Lam. 3:22–26)! I pray, Lord, that when You come again I will hear You say, "Well done, good and faithful servant" (Matt. 25:21). Please give me the power of the Holy Spirit to resist sin, and to live a life holy and pleasing to You. I need You to help me live out the fruit of faithfulness. Help me to be a person of integrity and truth. In the faithful and powerful name of Jesus I pray. Amen.*

Chapter 8

The Fruit of Gentleness

**Take My yoke upon you and learn from Me, for
I am gentle and lowly in heart, and you will find
rest for your souls.**

—Matthew 11:29

Scripture: John 21

A gentle breeze blows across the shore. The disciples are resting, but one of them, Peter, fixes his gaze on the horizon as the sun begins to fall behind the hills. He has dark circles of weariness under his eyes, and his heart is filled with despair. He has not slept well since the night he betrayed Jesus. Every time he lies down to rest he hears the rooster crowing and sees the hurt in the face of the One he loves the most.

Why didn't I stand up for Him? Why am I so weak? How could He ever take me back? Will things ever be the same again? These questions torment Peter as he watches the sun go down. He looks around at the other disciples and sees no anguish upon their faces. They will never trust me again, he grieves. They have lost respect for me!

As Peter glances at his friends, he recalls how they had all fled except John. What a bunch of weaklings! Why did Jesus choose us? He begins to feel better about himself because the others had deserted Christ too, until he sees John leaning against a tree. John had followed Jesus to the end. Peter is filled with envy as he thinks about the pleasure the Lord has found in John's faith.

Peter looks out at the Sea of Galilee. He remembers the time Jesus walked on the water and invited him to come to Him. When he began to sink, the Savior's hand was so gentle as He pulled him out of the raging sea. His mind looks back even further at the hope-inspiring time they met. These memories and his present despair are jumbled together as he waits here to see Jesus. What will I say to Him when He comes? he wonders. I'm so ashamed! I miss Him so much!

The other disciples are worried about Peter. His torment is obvious, and they know he has not been sleeping or eating. Their minds are filled with questions about the reason Jesus asked to see Peter here. What will Jesus do? Will He rebuke Peter? Will He be angry with him? Will He punish him?

Peter cannot stand the suspense any longer. He is tired of waiting, and he has to do something. Rising to his feet, he blurts out, "I'm going fishing." The other disciples look at him in amazement, but quickly gather to his side. They aren't going to let him out of their sight, and they all get into the boat and head out to the sea.

They fish all night, but catch nothing. Things are not much better on the sea than they were on the shore. All eyes are on Peter, but there is nothing to say. The silence is deafening.

As sunlight begins to break over the hills of Galilee, the disciples notice a figure on the shore. He calls to them and asks if they have any fish. When they tell Him no, He cries out, "Cast the net on the right side of the boat, and you will find some." At this point the disciples are ready to try anything, and they obey His word. Almost immediately the net is so full of fish that the disciples are not able to draw it in.

John looks at Peter and says, "It is the Lord!" He beams with joy as he watches Peter grab his outer garment and plunge into the sea. The other disciples follow behind in the boat, dragging their net of fish.

When they reach the shore, they notice that Jesus has prepared breakfast—fish cooked on a fire of coals and fresh bread. Peter is on his knees, clinging to the Savior, who is gently resting His nail-pierced hands on Peter's back. The disciples quickly leave the boat and run to Jesus. His face is filled with love and compassion as He greets each disciple with a hug and offers gracious encouragement. They sit down to eat together and once again enjoy the fellowship of the King.

As they finish breakfast Jesus looks to Peter and asks, "Simon, son of Jonah, do you love me more than these?"

The disciples are amazed at the question. How can Jesus ask such a question? Shouldn't He be enraged that Peter, our leader, left Him at the time of His torturous trial? How can He ask if Peter loves Him? Didn't his actions answer that question? How can Jesus be so gentle?

Jesus, however, can see what is in Peter's heart. He knows the sorrow and grief Peter feels and his deep desire to please Him. He is not surprised when Peter answers, "Yes, Lord; You know that I love You."

As Peter looks intently into the smoking coals, Jesus says, "Feed My lambs."

The other disciples are amazed at the gentleness of Jesus as He speaks again to Peter and asks, "Simon, son of Jonah, do you love Me?"

Peter glances at Jesus with confusion but says, "Yes, Lord; You know that I love You."

"Tend My sheep," Jesus replies.

Tears begin to flow from Peter's eyes as, for the third time, he hears Jesus ask, "Simon, son of Jonah, do you love Me?"

He rises to his feet and cries, "Lord, You know all things; you know that I love You."

As Jesus stands and looks into Peter's eyes, He again replies, "Feed My sheep." They embrace, and Peter feels the compassion and favor of God. His mind returns to the night of Jesus' arrest—his words of denial and the rooster's crowing—and suddenly the Savior's questions make perfect sense. He denied Jesus three times, and now he has been restored three times. He has been forgiven and commissioned to feed the Good Shepherd's sheep.

∾

Jesus' response to Peter's denial is a monument to the beauty of gentleness. Although He could have expressed righteous anger, He chose to be gentle. He could have rejected Peter at the shore and sent him away before the others reached land, but He did not. Jesus knew that Peter was sorry and really loved Him in his heart of hearts. Jesus chose gentleness!

This act of gentleness had a far-reaching impact. Jesus saw the repentance in Peter's heart, had mercy on him, and received him with open arms. His gentleness restored Peter to the fellowship of God's people and led him to the upper room. It was there that Peter received the power to please God with a life of holiness and dedication. In the upper room the Holy Spirit filled Peter to overflowing and gave him the strength to conquer his fears. Peter preached on the Day of Pentecost, possibly in front of those who had made him so fearful before, and three thousand people gave their hearts to Jesus.

After Peter surrendered himself to the Holy Spirit in the upper room, he received the power not only to proclaim Christ, but also to die for Him. Drawing on the ministry of the Holy Spirit, this one who had previously denied Jesus found courage to give his all. Peter preached the gospel of Jesus until it cost him his life. However, he is actually more alive now than he ever was on earth.

The life of Jesus was marked with gentleness and grace, and God wants to fill us with the fruit of gentleness. Ephesians 4:1–2 commands us to "walk with all lowliness and gentleness." First Timothy 6:11 says that we are to pursue gentleness, and Philippians 4:5 teaches that we are to let our "gentleness be known to all men." The apostle Paul wrote to the Christians at Thessalonica and said, "But we were gentle among you, just as a nursing mother cherishes her own children" (1 Thess. 2:7).

The fruit of gentleness is a work of the Holy Spirit. Is it any wonder that the Holy Spirit is called the Comforter (John 14:16, 26, KJV and ASV)? Just as Jesus continually comforted His disciples, the Comforter also embraces the people of God today. Under Christ's gentle nail-pierced hands we find ourselves baptized into the comfort of the Comforter. Under the power of the Holy Spirit we find the strength to lose our lives that we might save them. Gentleness is the way of the cross.

> *Lord Jesus, I want to surrender my all to You, but I feel like Peter. I do not have the strength. Unleash the power of Pentecost in me (Acts 2). Send Your Spirit to fill me with the strength I need to live for You and You alone! I surrender to You, Holy Comforter, come and lead me into the abundant life. Please fill me to overflowing with Your power and presence. May I live a life of love, gentleness, and grace for Your glory. In the powerful name of Jesus I pray, Amen.*

Chapter 9

The Fruit of Self-Control

**But put on the Lord Jesus Christ, and make no
provision for the flesh, to fulfill its lusts.**

—ROMANS 13:14

SCRIPTURE: MARK 5:21–43

Jairus wipes the sweat from his brow as he hurriedly shows
Jesus a shortcut through the back streets. They are heading to
his home so Jesus can heal his daughter. *I know there's something different about this Man,* Jairus thinks, his heart filled
with hope. *I know He can heal my little girl. I just pray that we
make it there soon enough.*

Jesus calmly follows the worried father. He could proclaim
healing for Jairus' daughter from here, but He wants to show His
compassion by visiting Jairus and his family. A crowd of onlookers begins to follow the two men. They know that synagogue
leaders have not been exactly friendly to Jesus, and they wonder
what this young miracle worker is doing with Jairus, the local
synagogue leader.

As the throng presses against the pair, Jesus suddenly stops
in the middle of the street. Turning around, He says, "Who
touched My clothes?"

The disciples look at the Master with confusion. "You see the multitude pressing in on You, and You say, 'Who touched Me?'" they ask.

Just then they notice a woman come and kneel at Jesus' feet. Trembling, she cries, "I'm healed. I've been so sick for twelve years, and I've seen every doctor in town. I've spent all I have seeking help, but You've healed me in a moment."

Jesus smiles at the woman and says, "Daughter, your faith has made you well. Go in peace, and be healed of your affliction."

Jairus looks on in amazement. Filled with joy, his heart asks, *Is this how He will heal my daughter?*

Just then, Jairus feels a tap on his shoulder. He turns, and as he looks into the face of an old friend, his smile quickly falls away. With tears in his eyes, his friend says, "Your daughter is dead. Why trouble the Teacher any further?"

Jesus, however, hears this, and He quickly says, "Do not be afraid; only believe." Forbidding the crowd to follow him any further, He takes only Peter, James, and John with Him to Jairus' house.

When they arrive, friends of the family are weeping loudly outside the home. The faithful from the synagogue have also gathered there. As Jesus enters the house, He asks, "Why make this commotion and weep? The child is not dead, but sleeping."

The crowd has not seen what Jairus has just witnessed, and the people begin to laugh at Jesus. Several of the synagogue members begin to mock Him. An anxious Jairus looks at the Savior and is amazed by what he sees. Even amid the ridicule, Jesus' face reflects confidence and self-control. Jairus can't believe the cruel derision of his friends.

Jairus looks through the bedroom door, and as he sees his daughter's limp arm hanging off the bed, his heart melts and his lips begin to quiver. Jesus and His disciples clear all the guests from the house, and Jairus feels his wife tugging at his cloak. They follow Jesus into the room where the little girl's body lies. Jairus can no longer hold back the tears as he looks upon her lifeless face.

Jesus sits on the edge of the bed, takes the child's hand, and says, "Little girl, I say to you, arise." At that very moment Jairus' twelve-year-old daughter stands up and walks, full of life! As the whole family—and even Peter, James, and John—leap for joy, Jesus turns to Jairus and instructs him to give his child something to eat. The synagogue leader reaches out and hugs Jesus with all he can muster. He will never forget the day he met God face-to-face.

∽

Can you imagine the self-control Jesus showed when the mourners at Jairus' house mocked Him? Wouldn't it have been harmless for the Son of God to reveal the most embarrassing moments of the men who were laughing in the corner? Surely it would have been all right to expose the lies and gossip of the women who were ridiculing Him? Why shouldn't Jesus confront the scoffing teenagers with their secret sins, or remind the cynical grandparents of their worst mistakes?

The Creator of the universe could have silenced the crowd of mockers with a miraculous sign or a glimpse of His glory. Instead He simply asked them to leave while He ministered to the family. Jesus is "no respecter of persons." He is concerned for all who hurt, and He desires to bind up all who are brokenhearted.

Isn't it amazing that Jesus asked Jairus and his family to keep the little girl's healing a secret? He could have had an earthly crown, but why would He want it? After all, He is the Lord of all creation, and His throne is in heaven. Jesus came to feed the hungry, clothe the naked, heal the sick, and save the lost. He came to set the captives free. Jesus was never out of control. He lived His earthly life under the control of the Holy Spirit, and it was a life of blessing.

The fruit of self-control is all about freedom. It is being free to do what is right and pleasing to God. We have no freedom without the work of the Holy Spirit in our lives! We need the freeing blood of Jesus, and we have nothing but bondage without submission to His will.

The enemy has tried to hide this truth by falsely presenting God's love letter as a rulebook and God's will as a curse. Second Corinthians 4:4 teaches that Satan has blinded the minds of those who do not believe, "lest the light of the gospel of the glory of Christ, who is the image of God, should shine on them." And 1 John 5:19 says, "The whole world lies under the sway of the wicked one." People who do not know Christ may reject the Word of God and think they are free, but they are only headed for disaster.

God has provided only one antidote to bondage; He has given only one solution for slavery. It is simply stated in 2 Corinthians 3:17: "Where the Spirit of the Lord is there is liberty." Living in the Spirit is the only way to be free from the sway of the evil one (Gal. 5:24–25). The fruit of self-control is found in the freedom of the Spirit-filled life.

> *Lord Jesus, I come to Your throne of grace today, asking for the fruit of self-control. Send Your Holy Spirit to minister true freedom in my life. I ask for the grace to submit to Your will more fully. Deliver me from the spiritual blinding of the enemy, and awaken my soul from his spells. Set my feet firmly upon Your truth, Lord Jesus, because I know that those You set free are free indeed (John 8:36)! May I love your will with all that is in me and also hate sin as much as You do! In the freeing name of Jesus, Amen.*

Conclusion

Abide in Me, and I in you. As the branch cannot bear fruit of itself, unless it abides in the vine, neither can you, unless you abide in Me. I am the vine, you are the branches. He who abides in Me, and I in him, bears much fruit; for without Me you can do nothing.

—JOHN 15:4–5

SCRIPTURE: JOHN 15:1–16

God desires that we be fruitful. In fact, Jesus says that we glorify Father God by bearing fruit. God does not want the branches of our lives to be barren and withered. He longs for us to reflect His own abundance for the glory of the Father, and this can only happen if we abide in Him!

Doesn't it seem significant that Jesus exhorted His disciples to abide in Him smack-dab in the middle of His richest discourse on the Holy Spirit in John 14:8–31 and John 16:1–15? Is it any wonder that Jesus' last teachings before His crucifixion directed His disciples to the Comforter who would transform them from within? Isn't this why Jesus came—to make it possible for the Holy presence of God to fill men and women?

The intended result of John 15 is not limited to the practice of believers abiding in Christ. Verses 4–7 also reveal the breathtaking reality of Christ abiding in us when we surrender to His lordship. Jesus died for our sins so the broken image of God could be restored in us. Because of His death and resurrection, we can experience the divine Spirit not only with us, but also within us. Jesus said:

> And I will pray the Father, and He will give you another Helper, that He may abide with you forever—the Spirit of truth, whom the world cannot receive, because it neither sees Him nor knows Him; but you know Him, for He dwells with you and will be in you.
>
> —JOHN 14:16–17

Jesus' teaching on the vine and the branches is as much about the sustenance of the Holy Spirit as any other scriptural truth. Without His sustenance, it is impossible to have a life of teeming fruit. John the Baptist proclaimed that Jesus would baptize us with the Holy Spirit. By submitting our lives to Jesus Christ we receive the ministry of the Holy Spirit, the sap that flows from the hands of Christ as He fills us and sustains us.

Before Pentecost the disciples only knew what life could be with a Helper. After Pentecost they discovered life, as it was meant to be, in the Helper. Isn't this the key? Life is so much more when God is resident and overflowing. Abiding in Jesus Christ through the Holy Spirit is the Father's dream for our lives.

This is the Good News of God! Jesus Christ died so we could receive the Holy Spirit and have Him in our hearts to lead us, guide us, and transform us into the people God has created us to be. The only way to abide in Christ is to submit to the leading of the Holy Spirit. No greater truth exists than the fact that those who place their faith and trust in Jesus Christ have the Spirit of God within them, preparing them for eternal fellowship with the blessed Trinity of God!

This is what the fruit of the Spirit is all about. The Holy Spirit desires to produce the fruit of righteousness in our lives so we will one day hear Jesus' words, "Well done good and faithful servant." Just as Jesus said, we cannot bear fruit apart from Him; we are also unable to experience the fruit of the Spirit without the ministry of the Holy Spirit. As we submit to His rule, He makes our lives a sweet aroma of purity and holiness before the Lord. The Holy Spirit is more than able to transform us and prepare us for the fullness of the kingdom of God.

The Holy Spirit has been called the "shy member of the Trinity." He desires to lift up the name of Jesus Christ rather than His own. As we read and study the Scriptures we need to pray that the Holy Spirit, who inspired the written Word, will open our spiritual understanding to know Jesus. In John 17:3, Jesus prayed, "And this is eternal life, that they may know You, the only true God, and Jesus Christ whom You have sent." The Holy Spirit desires to make Jesus Christ known to us, and He also wants to produce in us fruit that will be pleasing to Him.

Jesus has promised to never leave us or forsake us. He has also given us another Comforter to teach us on the path of the fruit of the Spirit. Our lives can be adventures in prayer as we seek the abiding presence of God and His holy will. We have the Bible as a prayer guide to lead us into Christ's pleasure and blessing so we can abide in Him and bear much fruit for the glory of the Father. This is the essence of the fruit-filled life, that we might please the One who has given His all for us.

Study Guide

INTRODUCTION

1. Have you noticed that one of the biblical names for the Holy Spirit is the "Spirit of Jesus?" (See Philippians 1:19; Romans 8:9; Galatians 4:6.) How does this make you feel? Names are significant in the Bible; they reveal a person's destiny and purpose. Notice the events related to the naming of John the Baptist and Jesus in Luke 2.

2. Think for a moment about the character of Jesus. Who is He to you? When you read the Scriptures, what do you appreciate most about His life? How does it feel to know that the "Spirit of Jesus" is with you today as you follow Christ? Read John 14:15–20. Be encouraged that this One you admire in the Word loves you and is forever with you!

3. The desire of the Holy Spirit is to "replicate the beauty of Christ in our lives." How do you think this happens? Read 2 Corinthians 3:7–18. How are we being transformed from "glory to glory"? Rest in the fact that you cannot mold yourself into the image of Christ. Only the Master Potter can mold you. God Himself is committed to your formation! He will replicate the beauty of Christ in you as you surrender to Him.

4. Consider the following statement: "It is impossible to
see Jesus for who He really is and not be forever changed."
Think about the times in your life when Jesus really
showed up. How did these experiences change your life?
How might you focus on Jesus this week? Remember,
you will be changed each time you truly meet with Him.
Maybe you have never experienced the love of Jesus
before. Why not ask Him into your heart right now?

Chapter 1

1. Read John 13:21–26, 36–38. Do you realize that Jesus
knew exactly what was going to happen to Him that
night and the following day? Jesus knew that Judas was
going to betray Him and that Peter was going to deny
Him. His prophetic anointing was so strong that He
could even see the rooster crowing.

2. Jesus grew up in the shadow of the cross. He had
read Psalm 22 and He knew from His favorite book
(Isaiah) that the Messiah would be a man of suffering.
I am sure he walked by men who were being crucified
on the outskirts of the city and somehow knew that He
would die the same way. Think about the fact that Jesus
could see the events immediately preceding Him and
still chose to face them because of His love for us. Do
not let that truth slip through your fingers!

3. Who is the most loving person you have ever met?
How did this person show care for you? How was this
person different from other people? How can you emulate
and implement character traits and actions that impacted

you in this relationship? There is nothing more meaning-ful in life than investing in the lives of others. How might you share the love of God with others this week?

4. Read Romans 5:5. Ask the Lord to fill you with His love for your family, your neighbors, your workmates, and your friends. The Bible teaches that God is love. He wants to make you an agent of love in this dark and hurting world.

CHAPTER 2

1. Read John 14:1, 18, 28. Our joy is forever linked to the degree that we trust God. If our trust in the Father heart of God slips, so will our joy. If the venom of doubt poisons our mind, our God-given joy will slip through our fingers until we learn to renew our minds in trust. How can you remind yourself daily to trust in God?

2. Luke 15 teaches that nothing gives God joy like the sinner who comes home. Renew your commitment to the Father today. Commit your life to sharing His life-changing love with everyone you meet. You will bring joy to both His heart and yours.

3. Look at 1 Timothy 2:1–6. What does this verse say about God? How should we live in light of this verse? Pray for your church today. Pray that God will empower you and your church to be a convincing witness for Jesus Christ.

4. Psalm 45:7, 46:4, and 92:4 identify key elements in finding joy. What are they? How can we express the joy of God in our daily lives?

CHAPTER 3

1. John 16:33 teaches us that peace is possible despite adversity and tribulation. Can you remember times when you have lived in peace despite trying circumstances? Are you going through a raging storm right now? Ask the Holy Spirit to help you face your trials with His peace. Remember that the joy of the Lord is your strength.

2. It is possible to be so attuned to your spirit that you can know the exact point when unrest enters your heart. Recall times when your peace has left. What triggered your lack of peace? How might you, with God's help, rise above similar difficulties in the future?

3. Our lives are so busy that it is very hard to set aside time to be alone with God and rest in His grace. Make a conscious effort to do this every day. We must find our center in God. Resting in Him is our only source of peace.

4. Take time to meditate on Philippians 4:6–7. Bring your requests before God, and realize who He really is. Record your prayers in your journal so you can remember to thank Him when He answers. Lay your burden and anxiety at the feet of Jesus. He will answer! Nothing is impossible with God.

CHAPTER 4

1. Romans 15:5 gives one of my favorite names for God—the "God of patience." How does it make you feel to know that God is patient? What are your favorite biblical examples of God's patience? Do you remember times when God was very patient with you? How can you relate to others with patience? You express your love for God practically when you show patience toward His people.

2. How do you handle times when it seems that God is silent? Choose to believe the truth that He loves you unconditionally, and trust Him with your struggles. Go to God in simple heartfelt prayer. Write your prayer in a journal and expect Him to answer. Read Psalm 90:4. God will answer your prayer in His timing. Do not forget to praise Him when He does!

3. Nothing can steal our joy like a lack of patience. Evaluate the times you have lost your patience. How could you have reacted differently? How can you demonstrate patience with your family, friends, and colleagues? Ask God for more patience as you pray today.

4. Read 1 John 3:2. Read it again, and let your finger pause briefly on each word. Let it sink in! God is not finished with you. He is constructing a masterpiece that will not be complete until you see Him face-to-face. You are not perfect, but be patient. One day you will be just as He wants you!

CHAPTER 5

1. Have you watched the power of kindness warm a cold, unloving heart? A genuine act of kindness can help bring a heart change to even the most callous person. Have you ever seen the friendly wave of a child introduce joy to a sad countenance? Commit your life to cheering others.

2. Is there a "Malchus'" in your life? Has someone consistently treated you poorly? Ask for God's grace to forgive that person. Ask for the power of the Holy Spirit to overcome anger and hatred through kindness. How could you show kindness to that person today?

3. As you read the Bible over the next year, make note of the times you see the kindness of God break through in the Scriptures. It is breathtaking to see the enormity and consistency of God's kindness in His Word.

4. Write out Romans 2:4 on the top of your prayer journal page. Ask God to bring your unsaved friends and family members to Christ. Pray that your loved ones will sense the amazing kindness of God and give their lives to Him.

CHAPTER 6

1. Do you know what is "written"? Have you, through memory, written the Word of God on your heart? Ask God to give you a scripture to memorize each week. You will be amazed as the power of God's Word transforms your life.

2. Read James 4:7–10. Ask God for the power of the Holy Spirit to resist sin. You are not alone in your battle against Satan. The Bible promises that if you resist the devil in the power of Christ he must flee. There is only one God, and the enemy must bow to the presence of Christ in you. He is afraid of Jesus, who lives in you!

3. Read James 1:12, and commit this verse to memory. Jesus knows the temptations you face. He will help you through your struggles. Do not try to resist sin in your own strength. Allow the Holy Spirit to give you victory over the power of sin.

4. Read Hebrews 4:14–16. Be assured that Jesus cares deeply for you. He is good and gracious, and He understands your struggles. Do not allow the enemy to sever your relationship with God, but heed the admonition to "come boldly to the throne of grace." God is committed to setting you free from all that binds you.

CHAPTER 7

1. Think of the following words: *durable, constant, steady, persevering.* What comes to mind when you think of these words? Do they describe your faith and character? Can your brothers and sisters in Christ count on you? How about your church or even more importantly the Lord Himself?

2. Faithfulness and consistency are the key to everything in life. What if you didn't show up one day as the parent of a newborn? What if you were unfaithful in your marriage? What if you shrunk away from all of your responsibilities? Praise God that He is always on time, and He always shows up! Thank God today for His commitment to you! He will always be there.

3. Read the following verses from the Book of Hebrews: 1:8–12; 3:14; 6:10–12; 7:16–17; 10:23; 10:35–39; 12:1–3; 12:26–29; 13:8. Spend time journaling with these verses in mind. Thank God for His faithfulness and ask Him for the grace to be faithful in your spiritual life.

4. Read Hebrews 10:19–23. In your time alone with God, reach out for all that He wants to do in your life. Allow Him to fill you afresh with His Holy Spirit.

CHAPTER 8

1. Have you, like Peter, failed miserably? Trust in God's gentleness, for He wants you back! He wants you by His side, walking in His Spirit. Christianity is more about who you are than what you do! God working through us is what really makes a difference in the world. James 4:8 says that if we draw near to Him, He will draw near to us. Claim this promise today and give your heart to Jesus afresh.

2. Just this morning I overheard a mother cursing her child. She said some very hurtful things to this little one because he spilled his drink. This is the very opposite of God's gentleness. If we only knew how hurtful words can be! Ask God to season your speech with grace and love. Ask Him to help you speak only blessing, joy, and encouragement into the lives of others. You can share the love of God very powerfully through the fruit of gentleness.

3. Have you ever thought of gentleness as a sign of weakness? If so, try being gentle in every interaction you have during the next week. If gentleness is a sign of weakness, why is it so hard to achieve? Gentleness is actually a sign of spiritual power and maturity.

CHAPTER 9

1. What do you think about the statement: "The fruit of self-control is all about freedom?" Do sins in your life keep you in bondage? The Holy Spirit has the power to set you free from the things that enslave you. God wants you to have the fruit of self-control.

2. Prayerfully read and apply 1 John 1:9. Do you need to repent of any sins in your life? The Greek word for repentance is *metanoia*, a word that literally means "to change the mind." Do you need God's power to overcome any sins in your life? Turn from them today and pray daily for the strength of the Holy Spirit to conquer sin. Do you know another Christian you can trust as an accountability partner? Find a Christian friend with whom you can pray on a regular basis. Help each other conquer the sins that drag you down (James 5:16).

3. Is there someone you need to forgive? Begin to pray for that person each day. Ask God for the strength to lay your bitterness down. You do not need to let that person's actions control your life; instead, allow God to cleanse away the hurt and anger that troubles your heart. Read 1 John 4:21. Ask the Holy Spirit to help you choose to forgive.

4. Read Psalm 119:9; Romans 12:1–2; James 1:12; 3:1–12. How has God spoken to you through these scriptures? Take a moment and record what He has said in your journal.

CONCLUSION

1. Think about the fruit described in this book. Which fruit seems to come most naturally to you? Which fruit is the greatest struggle? Commit to reading the Book of Mark over the next week. As you read the story of Jesus' earthly life record the stories that move you most. What fruit is displayed in Jesus' life? Pray that God will impart that fruit in your life.

2. Prayerfully consider the word *abide*. What does it mean to abide in Christ? I want to encourage you to live your life in God. One of the apostle Paul's favorite terms was "in Christ." Determine to live each day in partnership with God. Begin each day in prayer, and invite Christ into every decision. Live moment by moment in an attitude of worship and thanksgiving.

3. This book has been an exercise in praying the Word of God and placing ourselves in the biblical story. Make this a constant and enjoyable part of your quiet times with God.